BLUE BANNER BIOGRAPHY

CC
SABATHIA

Russell Roberts

Mitchell Lane
PUBLISHERS

P.O. Box 196
Hockessin, Delaware 19707
Visit us on the web: www.mitchelllane.com
Comments? email us: mitchelllane@mitchelllane.com

Mitchell Lane
PUBLISHERS

Printing   1   2   3   4   5   6   7   8   9

Blue Banner Biographies

Alicia Keys	Gwen Stefani	Megan Fox
Allen Iverson	Ice Cube	Miguel Tejada
Ashanti	Ja Rule	Nancy Pelosi
Ashlee Simpson	Jamie Foxx	Natasha Bedingfield
Ashton Kutcher	Jay-Z	Orianthi
Avril Lavigne	Jennifer Lopez	Orlando Bloom
Beyoncé	Jessica Simpson	P. Diddy
Blake Lively	J. K. Rowling	Peyton Manning
Bow Wow	Joe Flacco	Pink
Brett Favre	John Legend	Prince William
Britney Spears	Justin Berfield	Queen Latifah
CC Sabathia	Justin Timberlake	Rihanna
Carrie Underwood	Kanye West	Robert Downey Jr.
Chris Brown	Kate Hudson	Robert Pattinson
Chris Daughtry	Katy Perry	Ron Howard
Christina Aguilera	Keith Urban	Sean Kingston
Ciara	Kelly Clarkson	Selena
Clay Aiken	Kenny Chesney	Shakira
Cole Hamels	Ke$ha	Shia LaBeouf
Condoleezza Rice	Kristen Stewart	Shontelle Layne
Corbin Bleu	Lady Gaga	Soulja Boy Tell 'Em
Daniel Radcliffe	Lance Armstrong	Stephenie Meyer
David Ortiz	Leona Lewis	Taylor Swift
David Wright	Lil Wayne	T.I.
Derek Jeter	Lindsay Lohan	Timbaland
Drew Brees	Ludacris	Tim McGraw
Eminem	Mariah Carey	Toby Keith
Eve	Mario	Usher
Fergie	Mary J. Blige	Vanessa Anne Hudgens
Flo Rida	Mary-Kate and Ashley Olsen	Zac Efron

Library of Congress Cataloging-in-Publication Data
Roberts, Russell, 1953-
CC Sabathia / by Russell Roberts.
    p. cm. — (Blue banner biographies)
Includes bibliographical references and index.
ISBN 978-1-61228-053-0 (library bound)
1. Sabathia, CC (Carsten Charles) — Juvenile literature. 2. Baseball players — United States — Biography.
3. African American baseball players — United States — Biography. 4. Pitchers (Baseball) — United
States — Biography. I. Title.
GV865.S17R63 2012
796.357092 — dc23
[B]
                                                                                      2011016779

eBook ISBN: 9781612281803

ABOUT THE AUTHOR: Russell Roberts has written and published nearly 40 books for adults and children on a variety of subjects, including baseball, football, memory power, business, New Jersey history, and travel. He has written numerous books for Mitchell Lane Publishers, including *Holidays and Celebrations in Colonial America*, *What's So Great About Daniel Boone*, *The Life and Times of Nostradamus*, *Poseidon*, *The Cyclopes*, and *Larry Fitzgerald*. He lives in Bordentown, New Jersey, with his family and a fat, fuzzy, and crafty callico cat named Rusty.

PUBLISHER'S NOTE: The following story has been thoroughly researched, and to the best of our knowledge represents a true story. While every possible effort has been made to ensure accuracy, the publisher will not assume liability for damages caused by inaccuracies in the data and makes no warranty on the accuracy of the information contained herein. This story has not been authorized or endorsed by CC Sabathia.

PLB

Every baseball player's dream is to play in a World Series, and for pitchers it is to throw the first pitch in the series. Sabathia made that dream come true in the 2009 World Series between the Philadelphia Phillies and the New York Yankees.

CHAPTER 1

Big Game!

*O*n a freezing October night in New York City, lefthander CC Sabathia (seh-BATH-ee-uh) stood on the pitcher's mound in Yankee Stadium and took a deep breath. When he exhaled, his breath was frosty and white. Placing his foot next to the pitching rubber, he peered in at the catcher. Sabathia nodded slightly, took his windup, and fired the pitch toward home plate. Thousands of cameras flashed as the crowd of over 50,000 people roared. The first game of the 2009 World Series was under way.

The 2009 World Series matched the best team in the National League, the Philadelphia Phillies, against the New York Yankees, the top team in the American League. The game featured two of the finest pitchers in baseball: Cliff Lee for the Phillies and Sabathia for the Yankees.

Sabathia had signed a seven-year, $161 million contract with the Yankees during the winter of 2008. It was the most money ever paid to a pitcher in the history of baseball, but the Yankees needed an ace to anchor their pitching staff, and in Sabathia they thought they had one.

Sabathia quickly showed the Yankees that they had spent their money wisely. During the 2009 season, his first with the Yanks, Sabathia won 19 games while losing only 8. He struck out 197 batters and walked just 67. He was even better during the best-of-seven championship series that decided which team would go to the World Series. He won two games while allowing the opposing team just two runs.

Thanks to his strong pitching, Sabathia was right where he, and the Yankees, wanted to be: the World Series. Getting into the series was one of the reasons that Sabathia had joined the Yankees, and it was a major reason why the team had spent all that money to sign him.

Unfortunately, Sabathia was not his usual dominating self this World Series night. In the third inning, Chase Utley,

Chase Utley was the Phillies' hottest hitter during the World Series, slamming a record-tying five home runs. Even a great pitcher like Sabathia had trouble getting him out!

Philadelphia's second baseman, slammed a home run to put the Phillies ahead. In the sixth inning he did it again. The Phils rode his homers to a 6-1 victory. Sabathia pitched seven innings, but he was not the fearsome hurler he knew he could be.

After the game, Sabathia told reporters, "I wish I could stand here and say it was just two pitches, but I was behind pretty much the whole game. I was able to battle back and make some pitches when I needed to, but that's not at all how I've been pitching in the postseason."

Several days later Sabathia was back on the mound. He started Game 4 of the World Series on November 1, with the Yankees ahead two games to one. Although he didn't get credit for the victory, the Yankees beat the Phillies 7-4 to close within one game of winning the World Series. Sabathia pitched much better in this game. The Yankees gave him four runs, and Sabathia battled, holding Philadelphia to just three runs until tiring in the bottom of the seventh.

> CC Sabathia was a world champion—not too bad for a kid from a rough area in California.

A few nights later in Game 6, the Yankees beat the Phillies 7-3 to win their 27th World Series championship. A big reason for their success was Sabathia. But you wouldn't have known it by what he said after the game. He told reporters, "We've got a bunch of talent in here and a bunch of guys who get along and play well together. This [World Series victory] is what happened."

CC Sabathia was a world champion—not too bad for a kid from a rough area in California.

Growing Up in Vallejo

Carsten Charles "CC" Sabathia was born on July 21, 1980, in Vallejo, California. He was named after his father. There were temptations for kids on the streets of Vallejo—drugs and violence—but CC ignored those things. He liked playing sports, which offered a way out of the rough world of the streets. Baseball was his favorite.

His mother, Margie, helped him sharpen his baseball skills. She would put on all the equipment that a catcher uses—glove, mask, shin guards, and chest protector—and have CC pitch to her after he came home from school. She was a ballplayer herself—she played in a fast-pitch softball league—so she knew the value of practice.

"We did that until I was about 12, and I started throwing too hard for her," he recalled to *Sports Illustrated*. "One day, I hit her right on the palm, and that was it. She threw her glove down and walked off."

His mother taught CC important lessons about how to act as an athlete. Sports are unique in that one day you may be wonderful, and the next, not so good. An athlete must learn to take the good with the bad. Sometimes CC would get

CC and his mother Margie have always had a close and supportive relationship. She cooks him dinners to celebrate awesome games.

mad when someone got a hit off him. Margie took care of that display of temper. "She would pull me off the field," CC told the *Sporting News*. "She'd just say, 'Let's go home. I've seen enough.' "

Even though CC steered clear of bad influences as a kid, he was no saint. As a teenager he used to party with his friends behind his mother's back. "My mom worked nights as a telephone operator at Travis Air Force Base," he told *Sports Illustrated*. "She'd leave at 11 P.M., come back at 8 A.M. — perfect party hours. We'd have big parties until 7:30 then clean up. She never caught us."

Another person who helped CC grow and mature, both as a baseball player and as a person, was his grandmother Ethel. She taught him to be humble and to respect others. "She would always tell me that there were other players that were just as good and working just as hard," CC told *USA Today*.

> CC could do more than just pitch. He could hit, too. In one game Sabathia hit a ball so far that it was never found.

His uncle Aaron, who was CC's youth coach, also helped him get better as a ballplayer. CC was particularly close to Aaron's son Nathan. The cousins played high school baseball together and talked all the time.

As word of CC's pitching talents spread, scouts representing Major League Baseball teams started showing up to watch him play. CC could do more than just pitch. He could hit, too. In one game he hit a ball so far that it was never found.

At Vallejo High School, CC played basketball and football in addition to baseball. By his junior year he was already 6 feet 6 inches tall and weighed 245 pounds. With that size, it was almost inevitable that he would play high school football. He did, and he was as good at it as he was at baseball. He was an all-conference tight end. CC enjoyed playing football too—his favorite team was the Oakland Raiders—so when the University of Hawaii recruited him and offered him a chance to play both football and baseball, it seemed like a dream come true.

However, there was no denying his love of baseball. In his senior year of high school, CC had a record of 6 wins and 0 losses. He struck out 107 batters in 67 innings, which is almost two strikeouts per inning. He also posted a microscopic earned run average (ERA) of 0.87. (An ERA is a baseball statistic that measures a pitcher's effectiveness. It is the number of earned runs divided by the number of innings pitched, multiplied by 9, since there are 9 innings per game. Thus, a pitcher with an ERA of 4.00 allows an average of 4 earned runs per game. The best pitchers have low ERAs.) CC was such a good pitcher in high school that the magazine *Baseball America* rated him as one of the top pitching prospects in Northern California.

In the 1998 amateur baseball draft, the Indians drafted CC in the first round.

The Major League Baseball team the Cleveland Indians knew he was a good prospect too. They had been scouting his performance. In the 1998 amateur baseball draft, the Indians drafted CC in the first round. He was the 20th pick of all the players in the draft from the entire country.

CC chose baseball over football and college. In June 1998, he signed a contract to play for the Indians. The kid from Vallejo who loved sports was going to get a chance to play Major League Baseball.

The Young Pitcher

Just because Sabathia had signed a contract with the Indians didn't mean that he would automatically get to play major league ball. Many, many hopeful young men sign a contract to play baseball, but most never make it to the big leagues. They find the game is much faster, the pitchers much better, and the batters much tougher than those in high school or college. Many just don't have enough skill to compete on a major league level. As Sabathia's grandmother used to tell him, as good as he was, there was always somebody just as good—if not better.

The way major league teams try to get young players ready to play for them is to have them sharpen their skills in the farm system. The farm system consists of a number of minor league teams, each with different levels of players. As soon as a player proves that he can compete at a certain level with one team, he is promoted to the next level with a different team. It is like climbing a ladder. If he is good enough, eventually the player is promoted to the top step of the ladder—the major league team.

No matter how good they are in school, most young professional ballplayers start out in the minor leagues, where they learn how to play the game like they do in the majors. Sabathia was no exception.

After Sabathia signed his contract with the Indians, they sent him to their farm system team in Burlington, North Carolina. He appeared in five games and pitched a total of 18 innings. His record was 1-0. However, in those 18 innings, he gave up 20 hits and 14 runs. He was quickly finding out that his high school days, when he was unhittable, were over.

"In high school I had great control, but I only had one pitch—fastball—and I threw every pitch down the middle because no one could hit it," he told the *Sporting News*. That type of pitching would never do in professional baseball. No matter how fast a pitcher throws, professional hitters will be able to hit the pitch. A pitcher needs to have more than one type of pitch to survive. Sabathia was learning that lesson.

In 1999, Sabathia played for three different teams in the Indians' farm system. He compiled a record of 5-3. In 68 total innings pitched, he gave up just 47 hits and 29 runs. He was starting to learn how to become a major league pitcher.

> He had temporarily forgotten all that he had learned in the minor leagues. He just reached back and fired the ball as hard as he could.

The following year he pitched for two teams in the Indians' farm system, and posted a record of 6-9, which at first glance does not seem that good. However, in 146 innings he struck out 159 batters — more than one batter per inning!

The Indians decided it was time to find out what they had in Sabathia. The club's manager and pitching coach wanted him on the major league team, so for the 2001 baseball season, they promoted him to their club.

Sabathia was understandably nervous in his first major league start. He pawed the mound with his spiked shoes like he was digging a garden. Then he proceeded to throw 28 straight fastballs for his first 28 pitches. He had temporarily forgotten all that he had learned in the minor leagues about pitching. He just reached back and fired the ball as hard as he could. He did not calm down until after he had left the mound in the fifth inning.

He bounced back, however, and by midway through the 2001 season he was cruising. There were still bad games, though. In one against the Oakland A's, he once again relied

A pitcher's grip on the baseball determines how the ball will move as he throws it. A different grip each time can turn a standard pitch like a fastball into several pitches, each with its own unique rotation.

too much on his fastball and the A's pounded him. In just three innings Oakland smashed three homers and scored seven runs against him.

During that game, as Sabathia was walking into the Indians dugout after being pulled from the mound, one of his teammates—Roberto Alomar—caught his eye and made a flipping motion with his wrist. In baseball terms it means "mix up your pitches"—throw them curveballs sometimes instead of only fastballs.

"I didn't realize I had to make an adjustment until it was too late," Sabathia told the *Sporting News*.

As the youngest starting pitcher in the major leagues, these were the lessons Sabathia was learning on the job. He

Sabathia and Slider, the Cleveland Indians mascot, stand for the national anthem.

proved to be a good student. By the end of the season, he had compiled an outstanding record of 17-5. His ERA was a bit high—4.39—but in 180 innings, he had struck out 171 batters.

Sabathia finished second to outfielder Ichiro Suzuki in the voting for the 2001 American League Rookie of the Year. Everyone in the Indians organization was glad that he had been brought up to play for them.

"What CC has accomplished [this season] is a testament to who he is as a person—his intelligence, his maturity," Mark Shapiro, an Indians team executive, told the *Sporting News*.

Sabathia had wowed them in 2001. Could he do it again in 2002?

Indian Ace

Professional sports are full of stories of players who are very good in their first year and then never reach those heights again. For pitchers it is especially hard to stay on top. When they first come up, they are new; batters have never seen them, and it is hard for them to hit against a new pitcher. However, by the second year the batters have seen the pitcher and know what to expect. The pitcher constantly has to make adjustments in his pitching—especially in speed and delivery—to stay one step ahead of the batters. Some pitchers can change, and some pitchers cannot. Which one would Sabathia be?

The 2002 season did not get off to a promising start for Sabathia. In May he was partying in a Cleveland hotel room with a few people who turned around and robbed him. The bandits took $40,000 in jewelry and $3,200 in cash. Sabathia was lucky he was not hurt or killed.

Sabathia's mother and father came to Cleveland. CC hadn't seen his dad very much since he was about thirteen years old. Now here they were to talk sense to their son. His father stressed to CC that his life had to change. The talk made an impact.

"It pointed me in the right direction because life could have gotten worse," CC told *USA Today*. "And it gave me a chance to connect with my dad. That was huge. I had to change."

For the 2002 season, CC's win-loss record was 13-11. However, it was in the next season that he really began to blossom as a pitcher. His record was 13-9, and his ERA dropped to 3.60. He was giving up almost one run less per nine innings. As a measure of how good he was pitching, Sabathia was named to his first All-Star team that year. Only the very best players are selected as All-Stars.

> *... it was in that next season [2003] that he really began to blossom as a pitcher. ... Sabathia was named to his first All-Star team.*

More life-changing events happened the next year. Sabathia married his high school sweetheart, Amber Williams, and their son — Carsten Charles III — was born in September. Earlier that year, Sabathia's father had been diagnosed with stomach cancer and was given just a few weeks to live. He kept fighting to live because he wanted to meet his grandson.

"I'm sure that's why he was holding on," CC told Mel Antonen of *USA Today*. "I know he was holding out to see my son. He fought for that." Shortly after seeing his grandson, CC's father died.

Throughout the next few seasons, Sabathia kept improving as a pitcher. In 2004 he posted a record of 11-10 and was again named to the All-Star team. His record for

CC and his family met Yo Gabba Gabba! in May 2010. Left to right: Cyia, Amber, Jaeden, and Carsten; Carter would be born later that year. CC values his position as a role model for both children and adults, and always takes time to meet his fans, talk with them, and sign autographs.

2005 was 15-10. By 2006 his ERA had shrunk to 3.22—the third lowest in the American League.

In 2007 Sabathia put it all together. He pitched 241 innings, posted a record of 19-7, had an ERA of 3.21, and struck out 209 batters while walking just 37. He was the winner of the American League Cy Young Award, which is given to the best pitcher in the league.

Sabathia has won many awards throughout his career, including the Warren Spahn Award, named for one of the greatest left-handed pitchers in baseball history. It is given to the best left-handed pitcher each season.

"I was surprised [to learn that I won the award]," the typically humble Sabathia told the Associated Press. But others weren't surprised.

"I think Cy Young would have been proud to see Sabathia win this award," Indians pitching great Bob Feller said to *USA Today*.

"CC has become the guy other people are going to want to be compared to," Indians pitching coach Carl Willis told the *Sporting News*. "He's going to be one of the best lefthanders ever."

As a pitcher, Sabathia had developed a spectacular change-up and slider to go with his fastball. With his size—6 feet 7 inches and 290 pounds—he was intimidating on the mound. When he threw the ball, he resembled a boulder rolling at super speed down a mountain. He had also become a leader in the Indians clubhouse with his casual, no-ego attitude and his pitching skills.

For one of the best pitchers in baseball, what was next?

"I think Cy Young would have been proud to see Sabathia win this award."
—Bob Feller on CC winning the CY Young Award.

In the middle of the 2008 season, the Indians traded Sabathia to the Milwaukee Brewers, who were trying to make the National League playoffs.

To New York

*I*n 2007, Sabathia had been part of a winning Cleveland team that had made the playoffs. But by July 2008, the Indians were struggling and Sabathia was having a subpar year at 6-8 and an ERA of 3.83. That month they traded him to the Milwaukee Brewers of the National League. The Brewers were trying to make the playoffs and felt that Sabathia would put them over the top.

In a remarkable three-month stretch, Sabathia did just that. With Milwaukee he posted a record of 11-2, with a minuscule ERA of 1.65. He practically dragged the Brewers into the playoffs single-handedly. The team lost in the playoffs to the Philadelphia Phillies.

Following the 2008 season Sabathia was at a crossroads in his professional career. His contract was up and he was now a free agent, which meant that he could sign a new contract with any of the 30 Major League Baseball teams.

The New York Yankees of the American League were also at a crossroads. They had a good team overall, but their pitching was weak. They needed a good, dependable pitcher—someone to be the ace of the staff. Sabathia fit the bill perfectly. The Yankees offered him a 7-year contract for $161 million. It was the largest contract ever offered to a pitcher in baseball history. After talking it over with Amber, Sabathia decided to sign the contract.

> "Number one, ace, is probably the easiest way to put it."
> —Yankees Manager Joe Girardi about CC Sabathia

There was a question of how well Sabathia, who was used to smaller cities such as Cleveland, would react to New York's intense media glare. But right from the start of spring training he took steps to prove that he was comfortable being a Yankee. He took the corner locker in the team's clubhouse, where he could see everyone. He brought fellow pitchers fishing or to basketball games. When other pitchers were cut from the team, he talked to them to make them feel better. By the start of the season, he was most definitely a member of the team.

Sabathia was given the honor of pitching Opening Day for the Yankees against the Baltimore Orioles. Ironically, it was one of his poorer games. He lasted just a little over four innings, giving up eight hits and six runs. The Yankees probably gulped and wondered about their investment.

They needn't have worried. By the season's end Sabathia was his usual dominating self, posting a record of 19-8, 197 strikeouts, and an ERA of 3.37. He was the leader of the Yankees pitching staff—the one who stopped losing streaks and won big games.

Sabathia signed with the New York Yankees before the 2009 season. Although some pitchers have wilted under the glare of the New York spotlight, Sabathia fit right in with both the fans and his teammates.

"Number one, ace, is probably the easiest way to put it," Yankee Manager Joe Girardi told *The New York Times*. "You get wins, you get outstanding performances."

In the postseason, Sabathia turned it up a notch. He won three games and was voted Most Valuable Player in the 2009 ALCS (American League Championship Series). Overall, including his two World Series starts, he posted a 1.98 ERA. Helped in large part by Sabathia, the Yankees won the 2009 World Series.

Most athletes need both skill and emotion to help them on the playing field. Pitching is an especially emotional undertaking, and it is not unusual to see a pitcher like Sabathia celebrating a critical out.

The following season saw Sabathia continue his excellence. He won 21 games and reduced his ERA to 3.18.

Perhaps his best game came in April. Pitching against the Tampa Bay Rays, Sabathia did not allow a hit over $7^2/_3$ innings. He prowled the mound like a big cat, firing the ball toward home so hard it looked more like an aspirin tablet than a baseball.

Winning the World Series is the pinnacle in professional baseball. In 2009 Sabathia was able to reach that goal and celebrate with the New York fans in a ticker-tape parade.

In the seventh inning came the play of the game. Tampa's B.J. Upton slammed a ball down the third-base line. It looked like a sure hit, but Yankees third baseman Alex Rodriguez dived, stopped the ball, then jumped up and fired it to first, just nipping Upton.

In the next inning the Rays got a hit, spoiling Sabathia's no-hit bid. Although he did not get the no-hitter, Sabathia had a sensational year. It was the first time he had won 20 games in a season in his career.

"CC's arguably the best pitcher in baseball," Yankees shortstop Derek Jeter told *The New York Times*. "He's the guy that you want on the mound."

Sabathia is a true family man. He lives quietly with his wife and four children in a New Jersey suburb. In 2009, he and Amber began PitCCh In, a charity to help inner-city children.

CC Sabathia has already accomplished a great deal both in his life and in professional baseball. The sky seems to be the limit for this man who turned his back on drugs and violence in his youth and dared to dream of a better life—and achieved it.

> "CC's arguably the best pitcher in baseball. . . . He's the guy you want on the mound."
> —Derek Jeter

CAREER STATISTICS

Year	Team	GS	W	L	IP	H	R	ER	HR	BB	K	ERA
2001	Indians	33	17	5	180.1	149	93	88	19	95	171	4.39
2002	Indians	33	13	11	210.0	198	109	102	17	88	149	4.37
2003	Indians	30	13	9	197.2	190	85	79	19	66	141	3.60
2004	Indians	30	11	10	188.0	176	90	86	20	72	139	4.12
2005	Indians	31	15	10	196.2	185	92	88	19	62	161	4.03
2006	Indians	28	12	11	192.2	182	83	69	17	44	172	3.22
2007	Indians	34	19	7	241.0	238	94	86	20	37	209	3.21
2008	Indians/ Brewers	35	17	10	253.0	223	85	76	19	59	251	2.70
2009	Yankees	34	19	8	230.0	197	96	86	18	67	197	3.37
2010	Yankees	34	21	7	237.2	209	92	84	20	74	197	3.18
Career		322	157	88	2,127.0	1,947	919	844	188	664	1787	3.62

(GS=Games started, W=Wins, L=Losses, IP=Innings pitched, H=Hits, R=Runs, ER=Earned runs, HR=Home runs allowed, BB=Bases on balls, K=Strikeouts, ERA=Earned run average)

1980	Carsten Charles Sabathia Jr. is born on July 21, in Vallejo, California.
1998	CC is drafted in the first round of the amateur baseball draft, 20th overall pick, by the Cleveland Indians.
2001	He makes his major league debut on April 8.
2002	He is robbed after a party in a hotel room and decides to turn his life around.
2003	He makes the American League All-Star team. He marries his high school sweetheart, Amber Williams. Their son, Carsten Charles III, is born. CC's father, Corky, dies.
2004	CC makes the American League All-Star team again.
2005	His daughter, Jaeden Arie, is born.
2007	He makes American League All-Star team again and wins the American League Cy Young Award.
2008	On July 7, he is traded to the Milwaukee Brewers of the National League. His second daughter, Cyia Cathleen, is born. At the end of the season, he signs a seven-year, $161 million contract with the New York Yankees.
2009	During the regular season, he strikes out 197 batters; he wins 19 games while losing only 8. The Yankees win the World Series.
2010	Sabathia's son Carter is born. Sabathia posts 21 wins for the season. The Yankees win the division but lose the League Championship Series to the Texas Rangers.
2011	In the off season, Sabathia cuts sugary breakfast cereals from his diet and shows up to spring training 30 pounds lighter.

FURTHER READING

Books

Christopher, Matt, and Glenn Stout. *The New York Yankees: Legendary Sports Teams*. Boston: Little, Brown Books for Young Readers, 2008.

Greenberg, Keith Elliot. *Derek Jeter*. Minneapolis: Lerner Publications Company, 2005.

Shea, Theresa. *CC Sabathia*. Milwaukee: Gareth Stevens, 2011.

Stewart, Mark. *The New York Yankees*. Chicago: Norwood House Paper Editions, 2008.

Thomas, Keltie. *How Baseball Works*. Toronto: Maple Tree Press, 2004.

Works Consulted

Antonen, Mel. "CC Looks to Put October Troubles Behind Him." *USA Today*, October 18, 2007.

D'Alessio, Jeff. "My Profile." *Sporting News*, April 13, 2009.

Feinsand, Mark. "CC Sabathia Loses No-hit Bid with Two Outs in the 8th; New York Yankees Crush Rays, 10-0." *New York Daily News*, April 10, 2010.

Greenberg, Steve. "CC Sabathia." *Sporting News*, September 17, 2007.

Kepner, Tyler. "An Ace Shows He's Worth Every Penny." *The New York Times*, September 29, 2010.

McNeal, Stan. "Babes With Arms." *Sporting News*, August 27, 2001.

Nightengale, Bob. "Family Tragedy, Robbery Changed CC Sabathia's Life." *USA Today*, October 16, 2010.

———. "Sabathia Trumps Beckett for AL Cy Young Award." *USA Today*, November 14, 2007.

Reiter, Ben. "CC Sabathia." *Sports Illustrated*, April 21, 2007.

"Sabathia Only Second Indians Pitcher to Win Cy Young." *Associated Press*, November 14 2007. http://sports.espn.go.com/mlb/news/story?id=3108321

"Yankees Win in Six." *2009 Sports Collector's Edition*, November 4, 2009.

On the Internet

Baseball Reference.com: CC Sabathia
http://www.baseball-reference.com/players/s/sabatc.01.shtml

MLB.com: CC Sabathia Stats, Bio, Photos, Highlights
http://mlb.mlb.com/team/player.jsp?player_id=282332

Official Site of the New York Yankees
http://newyork.yankees.mlb.com/

Official Web Site of CC Sabathia
http://www.ccsabathia52.com

INDEX